POISONERS AND PRETENDERS

BY MICHAEL CHINERY

🌳 CRABTREE

4

577.34
Chinery

Crabtree Publishing Company

PMB 16A, 350 Fifth Avenue
Suite 3308
New York, NY
10118

612 Welland Avenue
St. Catharines, Ontario
Canada L2M 5V6

Created by
Cherrytree Press

© Evans Brothers Limited 2000

Library of Congress Cataloging-in-Publication Data

Chinery, Michael.
     Poisoners and pretenders / by Michael Chinery.
          p. cm.– (Secrets of the rainforest)
Summary: Describes the various defense mechanisms used by caterpillars, frogs, snakes, and other animals to fend off hungry predators.
     ISBN 0-7787-0219-7 (RLB) – ISBN 0-7787-0229-4 (pbk.)
     1. Animal defenses–Juvenile literature. [1. Animal defenses.] I. Title.
QL759 .C52 2000
591.47–dc21

Rain forest animals

                                        LC 00-021523
                                             CIP

Co-ordinating Editor: Ellen Rodger

Designed and produced by
A S Publishing
Editor: Angela Sheehan
Design: Richard Rowan
Artwork: Malcolm Porter
Consultant: Sue Fogden

Acknowledgements
Photographs: *All by courtesy of
Michael & Patricia Fogden*

123457890
Printed in Hong Kong by Wing King Tong Co. Ltd. 543210

❖ CONTENTS ❖

POISONERS AND PRETENDERS

RAINFORESTS grow in wet parts of the world, particularly in the **tropics** around the **equator** where it is hot all year round and it rains almost every day. More plants and animals live in the rainforests than anywhere else on earth. Many of them have ways of defending themselves against their enemies. Some rainforest animals, such as wasps, spiders, and many snakes, also use poison to capture their **prey**. Some animals get their poisons from the plants they eat. Other animals make the poison inside their bodies.

With so many animals ready to eat them, many smaller animals **evade** predators by staying still and blending in with their background. This **camouflage** also protects larger animals. Other animals pretend to be fierce, or they protect themselves by being a lookalike. Lookalikes, known as **mimics**, look like much bigger or more dangerous animals. **Predators** leave them alone because of their appearance.

POISONS AND PEOPLE

• •

THERE are thousands of different poisonous animals in the rainforests, such as this spider (left) which has sunk its fangs into a **katydid**. Very few animals are really dangerous to people, so you can walk through a rainforest without fear. Many rainforest plants are poisonous, but a lot of the poisons they contain become medicines when used in small doses. Rainforest peoples have known about these medicines for a very long time. Curare, from the bark of a South American tree, is a medicine used in operations. It relaxes the patient's muscles and allows the surgeon to work properly. Many other precious substances probably lie undiscovered in the rainforests and that is one reason why we must look after the forests.

◀ **Disguised as part of the plant, this katydid, a kind of cricket, waits for its prey.**

▼ **This monster-like insect is another katydid. It frightens away predators by looking fierce.**

▲ **Few animals attack bumblebees because of their stingers, but this is not a bee: it is a moth pretending to be a bee.**

POISONOUS OR VENOMOUS

Many poisonous animals have their poisons spread throughout their bodies. These animals do not taste good and may be dangerous to eat, but they do not attack other animals. Their poisons are used to defend themselves from attack. Other animals store their poisons in specific parts of their bodies. These poisons are called **venoms** and the animals usually have stingers or other ways of injecting the venoms into their victims. Animals with poisonous stingers are known as **venomous** animals, to distinguish them from those that are simply **poisonous** to eat.

Some animal venoms are simple acids that hurt or burn where the animal stings or bites the body. They only effect the area stung and soon wear off. Many ants deter their attackers by spraying them with formic acid. Most animal venoms are more complex. Some venoms affect the victim's nervous system, making it harder to breathe or stopping the blood circulation. Some animal venoms destroy blood cells or cause the blood to **solidify** in the victim's veins and arteries. Other venoms destroy the skin and other tissues around the wound.

⊛ Danger Beware! ⊛

HAVING A poisonous body or a disgusting taste is a good form of defense, but even the strongest poison is useless if an animal has to be bitten and killed or injured before a predator discovers that it does not taste very nice. Most animals that rely on unpleasant tastes for protection have ways of **advertising** the fact. They have bright colors or bold patterns that are known as **warning coloration**. Black and yellow are common warning colors, as are black and red, and black and white. Some animals use brighter or more dramatic color combinations, but the important thing is that they are eye-catching and memorable.

Eat Me if You Dare

Experiments show that young, inexperienced animals will eat anything they can, but they spit out things that taste bad. Predators soon learn to link bold color patterns with bad taste or getting stung. After that they leave those animals alone. Some prey animals have to die before the predators have learned their lessons but the warning colors do benefit the prey species as a whole.

▲ Many animals protected by warning colors also have nasty smells. This moth gives off a foul-smelling poisonous foam when it is bothered.

▶ The fire-bellied toad hides its brightest colors until danger looms. Their sudden appearance deters predators.

NATURAL SELECTION

NATURAL selection is the force that guides **evolution** and ensures that living things are **adapted** to their surroundings. It works because animals that are not well suited do not survive: they are caught and eaten or they die from disease or starvation. Animals with better camouflage or more poison survive to breed, and pass on their good qualities to the next generation. The process, repeated over and over, results in the protection getting better and better. The ancestors of this Amazonian caterpillar (right) probably had only mildly poisonous spines, but predators removed the least poisonous individuals in each generation and the insect gradually acquired the vicious spines it has today – as a result of natural selection.

Many insects with warning colors have tough skins that prevent them from being killed when they are attacked. Some also have bodies that heal quickly, so the number of animals that die before their predators learn to leave them alone is low.

▼ Warning coloration works so well that insects like this moth often rest openly on plants and make no attempt to escape if disturbed.

HARMLESS MIMICS

You do not have to be poisonous to gain protection from your enemies. Many harmless rainforest species deceive their enemies simply by looking like poisonous species. Having learned the hard way to leave poisonous species alone, the predators also ignore other animals with similar colors or patterns. This kind of trickery is called **mimicry**. The poisonous species are known as **models**, and the harmless tricksters as **mimics**.

Many bees and wasps are models and advertise their **stingers** and unpleasant tastes with yellow and black warning colors. They are copied by many harmless mimics, including moths, beetles and flies – particularly hover-flies. Many **edible** butterflies also mimic poisonous species, especially in the tropical forests.

The poisonous models are usually more numerous than their mimics. This ensures that most birds and other predators meet more models than mimics, so they learn that the bold patterns are associated with unpleasant experiences. If the edible or harmless mimics were more common than the poisonous species, the predators would find that most of the boldly marked insects actually tasted good. The system would then not work because all the insects would be attacked and none of them would benefit.

MIMICRY RINGS

THESE two butterflies look alike and they both taste awful, but they are not closely related. They actually belong to two very different families. They form part of a **mimicry ring**, which may contain a lot of poisonous insects with similar colors or patterns.

All the insects in the ring benefit because, once a predator has learned to recognize the warning coloration, all the species sharing it are protected. Only a few members of each species are killed before the predators learn the lesson, and the more species there are in each ring the better, because fewer members of each will die.

▲ The venomous coral snake (top) is a danger to other animals. It is the model for the harmless fire-bellied snake that mimics it.

HOW MIMICRY DEVELOPED

Mimics do not set out to copy their models. Mimicry, just like camouflage (see page 24), has evolved through the processes of natural selection. At one time, the similarities between the mimic and model would not have been very great, but even a slight resemblance to a poisonous model can help a mimic to escape by causing a predator to hesitate for a split second. Over many generations, the mimicry gradually improved and produced today's amazing similarities. Even people who know the differences often have difficulty identifying mimics and models.

◀ This animal looks like a wasp, but it is really a glasswing moth that protects itself by looking like a wasp.

❁ CREEPY CATERPILLARS ❁

SOME OF THE smallest animals in the rainforest are the most poisonous. Tropical rainforests are warm all year round. Butterflies, moths, and many other creatures, breed in rainforests all year long. There are millions of butterfly eggs and caterpillars. Caterpillars are soft and juicy, the perfect food for birds and many other predators.

For protection against these enemies, many caterpillars have poisonous fluids in their bodies and bright warning colors. Some smell bad as well. These caterpillars often live in clusters, making their colors and smells even more noticeable. Predators keep well away from them. Many other caterpillars have real weapons that can inflict painful wounds if they are attacked.

IRRITATING CATERPILLARS

Hairy or spiny coats make many caterpillars difficult or painful for predators to swallow. If they are attacked, the caterpillars may flick their bodies from side to side and try to drive the spines into the faces of their enemies. This can be very painful for monkeys and other small animals. Some spines and hairs are hollow and full of venom. Their pointed tips penetrate the skin and then snap off to release the stinging venom. All hairy caterpillars should be handled with care. The caterpillars of some South American silkmoths have venomous bristles that can cause severe bleeding even if you just brush your hand over them.

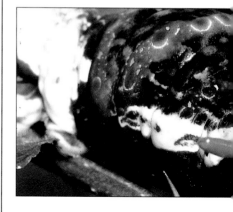

SWALLOWTAIL ATTACK

WHEN a swallowtail butterfly caterpillar is attacked, a forked sausage-like swelling called an **osmeterium** bursts out from behind its head. It is usually brightly colored and its sudden appearance is enough to frighten small birds. The caterpillar's acidic **secretions**

▼ This hairy tussock moth caterpillar may look pretty, but its hairs can hurt predators and humans.

▶ To predators, these caterpillars, clustered together, must look even more frightening than they would all alone.

▶ The spines of this venomous silkmoth caterpillar have tips that penetrate the skin like a hypodermic needle and snap off.

also irritate the birds' eyes. The osmeterium also gives out a strong scent, with each swallowtail species having its own particular smell. This is often pleasant to human noses, but it repels insect predators, including the **ichneumons** that lay their eggs on caterpillars. The insect larvae feed on the caterpillar body.

Some caterpillars incorporate their hairs into the silken **cocoons** that they spin before turning into pupae. When large numbers of moths emerge from their cocoons at the same time, they scatter millions of the poisonous hairs into the air as they fly. The hairs keep predators away. They also cause outbreaks of rashes and sore throats among humans living near the rainforest. Many tropical caterpillars surround their pupation sites with hairs as a protection against ants, which are major enemies of **pupae** in tropical areas.

FIRE BEASTS

SOME South American caterpillars are known as guinea pig caterpillars because their long, shaggy coats make them look like miniature guinea pigs. These caterpillars are very dangerous. The venomous spines hidden among their long hairs can cause severe headaches and serious damage to the skin in humans. The caterpillars are known as 'fire beasts' in some rainforest areas because their hairs produce such a severe burning sensation.

❂ SPIDERS AND STINGERS ❂

SPIDERS KILL their prey with venom produced in glands in the front part of the body. When the spider bites, the venom is pumped out through the **fangs** with great force. Spiders live everywhere in tropical forests. Huge webs, some three feet (one meter) across, stretch from tree to tree and their silk is so strong that they do not always break when a person walks into them. Birds are often caught in the webs. Most web-spinning spiders do not eat birds and many webs are spun in bold warning colors of red or yellow on a black background. This helps birds see the web and avoid damaging it by flying into it. Some spiders also have long spines that prevent birds from eating them.

TARANTULAS
Not all rainforest spiders make webs. Some are hunters. The bird-eating spiders, often called tarantulas, nest on the forest floor and come out at night.

▼ **This spider looks like a colorful jewel and could be mistaken for a flower bud.**

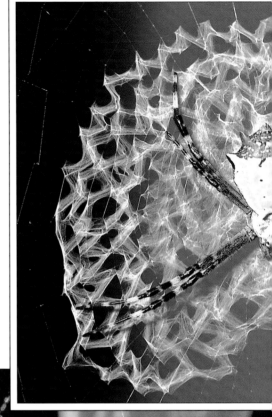

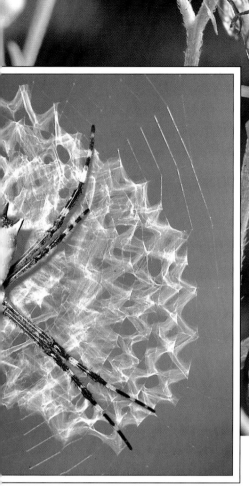

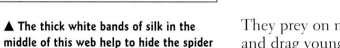

▲ The thick white bands of silk in the middle of this web help to hide the spider from hungry birds.

▲ Hidden in a cluster of flowers, this crab spider has caught a bumblebee.

They prey on mice and lizards. Some tarantulas climb trees and drag young birds from their nests. They have huge fangs, but they are not generally dangerous to people. Some of the smaller spiders are much more poisonous.

CRAB CAMOUFLAGE

Crab spiders sit motionless on plants or on the ground and seize any insect that comes within reach of their big front legs. They are usually so well camouflaged that their victims are unaware of the danger. Some crab spiders look just like bird droppings. This disguise protects them from birds and also helps them to find food. Butterflies and other insects often feed on bird droppings and other dung to get the salt they need. If they land on one of the bird-dropping spiders, it is usually the last thing they do.

◄ This hairy bird-eating spider, or tarantula, looks terrifying but its irritating hairs are more harmful to humans than its bite.

Venomous Centipedes

Centipedes are fast-running predators. Many species live in rainforests, on tree trunks and branches as well as on the ground. The biggest ones are about 12 inches (30 cm) long and they eat lizards, birds, and small mammals as well as insects and spiders. Their weapons are a pair of venomous fangs that curve around the head. Venom is produced in the base of each fang and is forced out when the fangs strike. Centipede venom is deadly to most small animals, and a bite from one of the larger centipedes is quite painful to people. The venom can cause blisters and may destroy the flesh around the bites.

Some large tropical centipedes can use their back legs to squeeze victims, as well as biting them with their fangs. They can even catch prey with their back legs. Both ends are brightly colored to warn enemies to keep away. Centipedes also have fluids that repel predators.

Bitter-Tasting Millipedes

Millipedes are slow-moving **herbivores**. Most of them can **secrete** bitter-tasting fluids from **glands** on their sides. These fluids protect the millipedes from predators, although toads can ignore the secretions. Large millipedes, up to 6 inches (15 cm) in length, can fire sprays or jets of fluid into the air.

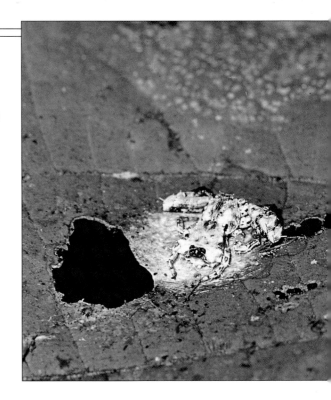

▲ Birds take no interest in their own droppings, so this spider's perfect disguise keeps it safe. Butterflies are enticed to feed on the 'dropping'.

▼ The lynx spider (left) is a hunter that runs down its prey. This pretty green one has caught a young plant bug.

STINGER IN THE TAIL

SCORPIONS are related to spiders but instead of fangs they have a stinger at the tip of their tails. Many scorpions live in rainforests, hiding away during the daytime and coming out to feed on insects and spiders at night. They also catch lizards and small **rodents**.

To inject its venom, the scorpion flicks its tail forward over its head at lightning speed and drives the stinger into its victim. Muscles in the bulb contract and pump the venom into the wound. Scorpions use their stingers mainly for protection, and sting their prey only if it struggles. This scorpion does not need to use its stinger. It has used its claws to catch its prey – a leaf-like katydid whose disguise has failed to protect it.

▼ **This long-legged centipede (center) is very fast and can easily catch spiders and beetles in the trees or on the ground.**

▼ **This giant millipede (right) feeds on dead leaves but its bright colors warn that it is very poisonous.**

These poisons can give rise to painful blisters and can cause blindness in any animal that tries to eat the millipedes. Some millipedes surround themselves with deadly cyanide gas when they are alarmed. The millipedes cannot store the poison in their bodies, so they make it in little pouches and fire it out of their bodies when attacked.

⚙ FEARSOME FROGS AND TOADS ⚙

FROGS LIVE at all levels in the rainforest, from the ground to the tops of the tallest trees. So much water is trapped in the vegetation that some kinds are able to live and breed in the tree-tops and never come down to the ground. Many of them have suckers on their toes that help them cling to the shiniest leaves. They are active by day and by night and they eat all sorts of insects, spiders, and worms.

SLIMY PROTECTION
All frogs are covered with a thin layer of slime that oozes from glands in their skin. The slime helps to keep the skin moist when the animals are out of water. Frogs breathe partly through their thin skins, but oxygen can pass through the skin only if it is moist. The slime of most frogs is also slightly poisonous and kills most of the **bacteria** that might damage the thin skin. This is why frogs can live safely in dirty ponds. When a frog is frightened, it pumps out extra slime, making itself extra slippery so that it can escape more easily if it is caught by an enemy.

FROG OVERKILL

THERE are about 100 different kinds of arrow-poison frogs in rainforests and most of them advertise that they are poisonous with their brilliant colors. The frogs are protected mainly by the awful taste of their skin secretions, which may also cause a burning sensation in the mouth. Predators immediately let go of any frog they pick up, and then remember not to touch any more frogs with the same bright colors. The secretions, or slime, coats the frogs' bodies, making it impossible for a predator to eat them.

▲ The blue arrow-poison frog (right) and the kokoe-pa arrow-poison frog (left) are among the most poisonous animals in the world.

◀ The skin of this bright little tree frog is almost translucent. The poisonous slime on its skin keeps it moist and free from germs.

▶ The toad-eater snake specializes in eating toads. It will even attack a toad that has puffed itself up to twice its normal size.

ARROW-POISON FROGS

A frog's slime is not usually harmful to people, but a few species produce extremely poisonous slime that can kill people if it gets into their blood. The most poisonous of these frogs live in the rainforests of South and Central America. They are commonly known as arrow-poison frogs because the forest people collect the poison and use it on their hunting arrows. These weapons quickly kill any animal that they hit. Even a tiny scratch can cause death. The poisons affect the nerves and muscles and cause **paralysis** and heart failure. But they act only when they enter the blood through a wound. They are destroyed by **digestive juices**, so animals killed by the poisoned arrows can be safely eaten by humans.

Some arrow-poison frogs are so poisonous that the hunters can pick up enough poison by rolling their arrows along the frogs' backs. Treated arrows remain poisonous for months.

◦ VENOMOUS SNAKES ◦

RAINFOREST are full of snakes. Some snakes are **venomous**. They kill their prey by injecting venom with enlarged teeth called fangs. The venom is also used for defense when necessary. Some non-poisonous snakes can also inflict painful bites with their dagger-like teeth.

ON FLOOR AND BRANCH

Rainforest snakes live in the trees as well as among the dead leaves on the ground. Many of those that slither through the tall trees are slender snakes that resemble lianas, plants that twist and coil among the branches of trees. These snakes are difficult to see, so it is easy for them to creep up on or ambush their prey undetected. Rainforest snakes have **prehensile tails** that wrap around tree branches and prevent the animals from falling when they strike.

Tree-living snakes are active mainly in the daytime and most of them are ambushers. They strike at prey whenever it comes within range. They need good eyesight for picking out lizards and other small prey among the branches.

▼ Unlike most tree snakes, the plain tree snake is nocturnal. It uses its big eyes to find its prey at night.

▲ An eye-lash viper holds tight with its tail while striking at a passing hummingbird.

Deep grooves in front of the eyes of the oriental whip snake allow it to see to the front as well as to each side. Several other slender, tree-living snakes have similar grooves.

Ground-living snakes are mostly night hunters or ambushers. They lie in wait for their prey or track it down mainly by following its scent. Pit vipers also home in on the warmth of their prey. Heat-sensitive pits on their snouts detect very small changes in temperature and tell the snakes when warm-blooded prey is near. The pits can guide the snakes towards their prey as accurately as eyes, and the snakes can then strike with amazing accuracy even in the dark.

▲ Coral snakes are the most colorful of the rainforest species. Although they have small fangs, they are very poisonous.

◄ Up to 13 feet (four meters) long, the bushmaster is the largest and one of the most venomous snakes in South America. It is a pit viper. Despite its size, its markings make it hard to see on the forest floor.

Come and Get It!

Some snakes lure their prey to their death by offering them some kind of 'bait'. Several species twitch their tails to attract birds. The African twig snake lures frogs and lizards by waving its orange tongue, which the prey mistake for a juicy caterpillar. The twig snake is well camouflaged at rest, but when it spots a frog or a lizard, it sticks out its colorful tongue to tempt the prey within range. It is one of the few back-fanged snakes that are dangerous to people.

Keep Away!

The boomslang, a tree-living snake from tropical Africa, is the most dangerous of the back-fanged snakes. A startled boomslang hisses loudly and puffs up its throat to twice its normal thickness, so that its scales stand out like bristles. This scares off most other animals. Cobras are famous for the way in which they expand their necks when they are threatened. Cobra puffing usually shows a startling mask-like pattern, with one or two eye-like markings.

Venom Control

SNAKE venom is produced and stored in special **salivary glands** in the roof of the mouth. The poisonous parts of the freshly made venom are packed into tiny round drops of liquid surrounded by thin layers of connective tissue. The poison itself is not released from these packets until the venom is pumped out, so the snake is in no danger of poisoning itself. Vipers can control the amount of venom they release. They usually inject smaller amounts of venom into their enemies than into their prey because they don't need to kill their enemies – just stop them. Sometimes vipers bite without injecting venom at all. Some, like this Sumatran pit viper, simply frighten their enemies away.

FANGS

VENOMOUS snakes belong to three main groups: vipers, back-fanged snakes, and cobras and their relatives. Vipers have long fangs at the front of their mouths. The fangs are folded back when the mouth is shut, but swing forward to strike when the snake opens its mouth. This hog-nosed viper (left) is ready to strike. Back-fanged snakes generally have small fangs at the back of the mouth and usually feed on small animals. They cannot open their mouths wide enough to sink their fangs into large creatures. The third group includes mambas, which have fairly short fangs at the front of their mouths but can inject their venom into their victims much more easily than back-fanged snakes. Coral snakes and cobras also belong to this group.

The pattern warns animals that might tread on the cobra by accident. The snake appears even more frightening because of the way it rears its head and moves it around to face any disturbance.

Green mambas are related to cobras. They are the slimmest of all the really poisonous snakes. The black mamba lives mainly on the ground and is the fastest of all poisonous snakes. It can reach 16 miles an hour (25 km/h) for a short while, although it is normally much slower. It can slide along with its head raised about 20 inches (50 cm) above the ground. Mambas feed mainly on lizards, birds, and small rodents.

▲ The gaboon viper has the longest fangs of any snake. They are about 3/4 of an inch (2 cm) long. The snake is hard to spot on the forest floor and hisses when large animals approach.

◄ The Indian cobra rears its hood as a threat, or in fear.

21

❂ BLUFFING IT OUT ❂

PRETENDING TO be much bigger or meaner than you really are is a good way to scare your enemies and make sure that they do not attack. Many harmless animals fool their enemies by displaying this kind of frightening behavior whenever they are disturbed. Large eye-like markings are a particularly good bluff, especially when the markings are revealed suddenly. Many moths raise their front wings when they are disturbed, and reveal large eye-spots on their hindwings. These eye-spots look like the eyes of much bigger animals, such as cats or owls. Several crickets, bugs, and mantises have these eye markings.

FALSE HEADS AND FALSE FACES

Many caterpillars have eye-like markings near the front of their bodies. These spots are small when the caterpillars are resting, but puff up when the caterpillar is alarmed.

▼ This hawkmoth caterpillar from Malaysia hangs upside down and frightens attackers by lunging at them. The markings near the front of its body look like eyes and the insect looks like a snake.

PLAYING DEAD

SOME animals pretend to be dead when they are disturbed. They become stiff and often fall to the ground motionless. In the rainforests, a variety of snakes, **stick insects**, and some butterflies and moths do this. As long as they remain absolutely still, they are safe because most predators are interested only in moving prey. It would take a sharp-eyed predator to see two moths among these dead leaves (above).

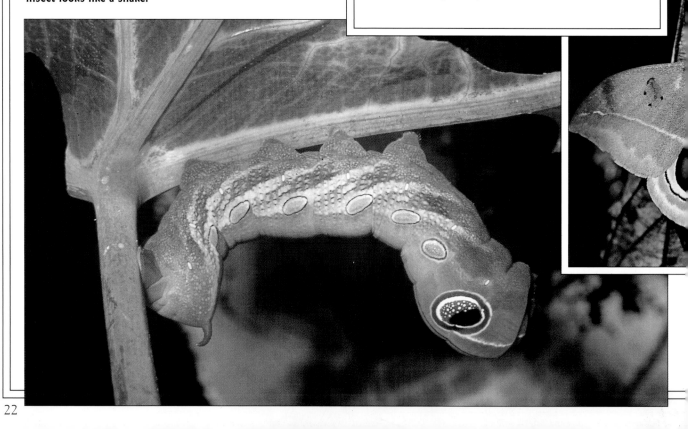

BACK TO FRONT

A NUMBER of butterflies and other insects have dark spots or other patterns at the rear of their wings. These can easily be mistaken for the insects' heads. Many of them also have thread-like outgrowths that resemble antennae. Birds and other predators are often fooled by these insects and they attack the wrong end. Instead of getting a nice juicy mouthful, all they get is a bit of a false antenna or wing as the insect flies off in the opposite direction. Can you make out which is the front, and which the back-end of this butterfly?

▼ When this silkmoth (center) is startled it opens its wings to reveal huge eye-spots that deter attackers.

▼ When this leaf-litter frog (bottom) is threatened it turns away and shows two large eye-spots on its rump.

When frightened, the caterpillar sometimes lifts its front end and moves it from side to side. Birds and other predators mistake the swaying caterpillar for a snake and leave it alone.

SOUNDS TERRIFYING!

Some mantises bluff their way out of trouble with the help of sounds. When a **mantis** is alarmed it raises its wings and then brushes its abdomen against them. The wings are quite stiff and the action produces a rustling or hissing sound. Many birds and other small animals seem to be frightened of hissing sounds and they back away, although the mantis is not really dangerous. The insect adds to its warning by showing bright colors or eye-spots. Several other insects, including various caterpillars and cockroaches, make hissing noises when touched.

❖ HIDE AND SEEK ❖

ESCAPING from enemies and avoiding being eaten is an important part of life for most animals. Some of them, especially animals that live in open country, rely on speed to get away from their predators. Some animals are protected by spines or other weapons. Other animals are poisonous or they pretend to be poisonous. Some animals even pretend to be dead. Most small animals escape their predators by using some form of camouflage. This kind of trickery uses colors and patterns to conceal the animals so that their enemies do not notice them.

Camouflage is particularly well developed in the rainforests, where large numbers of animals are trying to find food and even more are trying to hide. The rainforest animals have **evolved** with some really amazing survival tricks.

BLENDING IN

The simplest way of hiding is to blend in with the surroundings, and this is exactly what many insects and other small animals do. Many caterpillars have exactly the same green color as the leaves on which they feed and they are very difficult to see.

Glasswing butterflies use a different method to blend in with their backgrounds. Their wings are almost completely transparent, so you can see the leaves or flowers behind them without even noticing the butterflies. Bark mantises can wait for their prey on tree trunks without being seen, and so can various geckoes and other lizards.

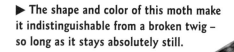

▶ **The shape and color of this moth make it indistinguishable from a broken twig – so long as it stays absolutely still.**

1

2

Guess what!

Can you make out the animals in these pictures? They may look like bits of plants but all of them are insects.

They are:

1. a bark mantis
2. two prominent moths
3. a stick insect
4. a lichen katydid
5. a praying mantis
6. an orion butterfly.

3

4

5

6

BREAKING UP OUTLINES

Larger animals also benefit from camouflage. Most deer and antelopes have a dark back and a paler underside, something known as countershading. The pale underside counteracts the shadows and helps the animal more easily blend in with its background.

The leopard's spotted coat looks like patches of light and shade and helps to camouflage the animal in the forest. The leopard has no enemies, but camouflage helps it to creep up on its prey without being seen. The tiger's stripes do the same thing by breaking up the outline of its body. The zigzag patterns of many snakes also help them to hide from their prey on the forest floor.

Patterns that break up an animal's outline are called disruptive patterns. They usually consist of two or more colors with sharp dividing lines between them. Predators' eyes are drawn to these boundaries and they do not notice the shape of the whole animal. Many moths rely on these patterns to break up their outlines when resting on tree trunks and other surfaces.

▲ A katydid from the South American rainforest is perfectly disguised as a shiny green leaf.

▼ The Asian horned frog is more likely to be stepped on than spotted on the forest floor.

▲ Perched on a branch, the potoo looks more like a gnarled stump than a bird.

▼ Transparent wings make this glasswing butterfly almost invisible.

LOOKING LIKE TWIGS AND LEAVES

Birds and other predators do not eat twigs or leaves and so they take no notice of insects that resemble them. Many caterpillars are twig-like, and often have little bumps that resemble buds. Some stick insects are even more twig-like. The insects nibble leaves at night and usually spend the daytime clinging to twigs. They even sway gently from time to time, as if being blown by the breeze. Their skins are often the same color as the twigs and this makes the insects very difficult for predators to see.

Leaf insects, which live only in Southeast Asia, are closely related to stick insects, but their bodies are flat and leaf-like. Flaps on their legs look like pieces of nibbled leaves. Rainforest **bush-crickets** also have some leaf-like species. The veins on their wings match those on the surrounding leaves and the wings often have pale spots that resemble the natural **blemishes** on the leaves. This form of camouflage in which animals resemble twigs and leaves or other objects in their environment, is called protective resemblance.

LOOKING LIKE FLOWERS

Mantises are long-legged insects that lurk among the rainforest trees. Most are green or brown and are well camouflaged among the leaves and twigs. Unless they are very hungry, mantises lie in wait for prey to come within reach of their spiky legs. Their prey is rarely aware of the danger. Other mantises are colorful, and are more likely to be found in flowers. Some look so much like flowers themselves that insects come to drink their nectar and find themselves being eaten instead.

COLOR-CHANGERS

Chameleons prowl slowly and almost unseen through the forest. These lizards are masters of camouflage. They can change their colors to match various backgrounds. Their bodies are flattened from side to side and often look leaf-like. They even sway on the twigs as if fluttering in the breeze.

Blue and yellow layers in the skin combine to give most chameleons an overall green color, but the animals can change this by altering the distribution of a black **pigment**. This pigment is contained in little packets with branches spreading through the surface layers of the skin. If the pigment is pumped into the branches, the skin becomes darker. If the process continues, the chameleon becomes almost black.

▲ This butterfly met its death in the claws of the flower mantis, which it did not see lurking in the flowers.

▼ The diamond pattern on this snake's skin breaks up its outline so that other animals cannot see its complete form.

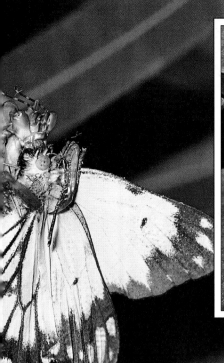

▲ This orchid mantis (right) from Malaysia looks as inviting to visiting insects as the flower on which it sits.

▼ Like chameleons, anoles can swiftly change their color. This one's skin is just like the branch on which it sits (below). Its colorful throat pouch is enlarged when it is excited or frightened.

If the pigment is drawn back into the packets, the chameleon's skin surface becomes pale. The color change takes just a few minutes and can produce almost all shades of yellow, green and brown.

As well as changing color to match different **environment**s, chameleons can change color according to their moods. When they are frightened, many species become almost black. This also scares their enemies. Some chameleons also puff themselves up with air when they are frightened. This makes them appear bigger and more frightening to predators.

❃ GLOSSARY ❃

Adapted Suited for a specific use.

Advertise To make an announcement of, make known, or call attention to.

Bacteria Small forms of life that play an important role in the breakdown and recycling of dead plants and animals. Many of them, often known as germs, cause disease in living plants and animals.

Blemishes Flaws or defects of the skin.

Bush-crickets Insects like grasshoppers, but with long antennae, that live in bushes and other undergrowth.

Camouflage Skin colors and patterns that help an animal blend with its surroundings and avoid the attention of predators.

Cocoon A silken bag that many caterpillars spin around themselves before turning into pupae, or chrysalises.

Digestion The process by which food is converted into energy by the body.

Edible Good to eat.

Environment Surroundings that an animal lives in

Equator An imaginary line around the centre of the earth mid-way between the north and south poles.

Evade To escape or avoid.

Evolution The process by which plants and animals slowly change from generation to generation, gradually giving rise to new species that are adapted to different habitats and different ways of life.

Experiments Tests under controlled conditions.

Fang Name given to any large tooth, but especially one that can inject poison.

Gland Any organ in the body that produces and releases substances for action either inside or outside the body. Digestive glands make juices to digest food, while venom glands produce poison to attack other animals.

Herbivore An animal that feeds only on plants.

Ichneumons Insects related to wasps that lay their eggs in the eggs or larvae of other insects, so that their offspring have fresh food when they emerge.

Katydids Various kinds of bush-crickets, especially in America. Many of them have evolved remarkable camouflage.

Leaf insects Insects related to stick insects that resemble leaves.

Mantis Member of a group of predatory insects related to cockroaches. Mantids have long spiny front legs.

Mimic An animal species that gets some protection or other benefit by resembling another species – called the model.

Mimicry A form of trickery in which a harmless or edible animal avoids being eaten because it looks like a harmful or inedible animal.

Mimicry ring A group of animals, not necessarily related, that benefit by sharing a similar pattern of warning colors.

Model A venomous or otherwise harmful species with warning coloration that is copied by other species, known as mimics.

Natural selection The weeding out of weak and inefficient individuals during the process of evolution. Because the weakest ones are removed in each generation – usually by predators – the population as a whole gets stronger and more efficient.

Osmeterium A fleshy scent gland possessed by various caterpillars. It is blown up just behind the head when the caterpillar is alarmed and it frightens predators.

Outbreak A sudden outburst or increase.

Paralyse To cause paralysis.

Paralysis Inability to move, sometimes brought about by poison.

Pigment Color.

Poisonous Something that can kill or harm.

Predator Any animal that hunts and kills other animals for food.

Prehensile tail A tail that can grip a support by wrapping around it.

Prey Any animal that is killed by another animal for food.

ENDANGERED!

RAINFORESTS are home to more plants and animals that any other habitat on earth. They are important to the world but they are in danger of destruction. Many of the animals and plants shown in this book are endangered. Their rainforest habitat is slowly being destroyed by humans. If you are interested in knowing more about rainforests and in helping to conserve them, you may find these websites useful.

Friends of the Earth
USA - *www.foe.org*
Canada - *www.foecanada.org*

Rainforest Foundation
www.savetherest.org

Rainforest Alliance
www.rainforest-alliance.net

Rainforest Action Network
www.ran.org

Greenpeace
USA - *www.greenpeaceusa.org*
Canada - *www.greenpeace.ca*

Environmental Education Network
www.environlink.org.environed/

◄ **The map shows the location of the world's main rainforest areas.**

NORTH AMERICA
EUROPE
ASIA
Tropic of Cancer
AFRICA
Equator
Tropic of Capricorn
SOUTH AMERICA
AUSTRALIA

Protective resemblance A form of camouflage in which an animal resembles a leaf or a twig, or some other object in which predators have no interest.

Pupa The stage in an insect's life during which it changes from a larva or caterpillar into an adult.

Rodent Any mammal belonging to the order Rodentia, which contains rats and mice, squirrels, and guinea pigs. Most of them are planteaters and all have sharp, chisel-shaped front teeth.

Salivary glands The glands in an animal's mouth that secrete saliva. The main function of saliva is to start the digestion of food. Snake venom is a special kind of saliva.

Secretion Substance produced and released by a gland.

Solidify To make solid, strong, or firm.

Stick insect Slender insect that resembles a plant stem or twig.

Stinger Sharp pointed structure at the end of the body, through which insects, such as bees and wasps, inject venom to paralyse prey and defend themselves. Scorpions also have stingers.

Tropics Hot or warm regions that lie between two imaginary lines, also called tropics, north and south of the equator.

Venom A poison that is fired at or injected into prey or an enemy.

Venomous Having venom, used for defense or to kill prey.

Warm-blooded Warm-blooded animals keep their bodies at a constant high temperature, no matter what the surrounding temperature may be. Birds and mammals are warm-blooded animals. Amphibians and reptiles are cold-blooded.

Warning coloration Bold or bright skin colors or patterns that warn predators that an animal is poisonous or has other unpleasant features.

❀ INDEX ❀